Getting Serious Buyers and Sellers Using AI

FUTURE-PROOF REALTOR

Martin Tijmes

CONTENTS

PREFACE:	WHY THIS BOOK MATTERS	5
CHAPTER 1:	NAVIGATING A SHIFTING MARKET - HOW TO FUTURE-PROOF YOURSELF IN SHIFTING MARKET CONDITIONS	9
CHAPTER 2:	MOVING AROUND-DOMINATING ANY MARKET WITH THE RIGHT STRATEGY	15
CHAPTER 3:	THE REMOTE REALTOR	27
CHAPTER 4:	FUTURE PROOF YOUR CAREER BY NOT BEING A SUCKY AGENT	37
CHAPTER 5:	THE GRASS IS GREENER WHERE YOU WATER IT	47
CHAPTER 6:	SELL HOMES SYSTEMATICALLY, DON'T BE THE COG	55
CHAPTER 7:	THE NEW WAVE OF REAL ESTATE WITH AI: CRM SYSTEMS	65
CHAPTER 8:	COMPREHENSIVE SUMMARY AND INSIGHTS	77
CHAPTER 9:	JOIN THE TEAM: WHY BEING PART OF THE RIGHT AGENCY MAKES ALL THE DIFFERENCE	83

PREFACE:

WHY THIS BOOK MATTERS

This isn't just another real estate book filled with tips and tricks. It's a blueprint for creating the kind of real estate business you've always dreamed of. Think of this as a mirror held up to your career—a chance to reflect on what's working, what's holding you back, and what's possible when you change your approach.

I didn't start out with a perfect plan. Like many agents, I was grinding day after day, chasing deals and hoping for the best. And like you, I've had my fair share of challenges, setbacks, and moments where I thought, *Is this really worth it?*

But I figured something out along the way: you can't keep hustling forever. The grind alone won't get you to where you want to be. That's when I made a choice—I stopped thinking about it as just selling houses and started to think about it as **building a business**. A business that uses smart systems, leverages AI to automate tasks and gives me the freedom to scale without burning **out.** And this book is about showing you exactly how to do that.

In this book, I'm going to break down the real obstacles standing in your way—whether it's your mindset, your systems (or lack of them), or the overwhelming list of tasks that pull you in a thousand different directions. You're going to see the truth about what it takes to be successful in real estate and more importantly, how to **future-proof** your career so you're not constantly grinding for every deal and being left behind. This is one big reason why I created the Accessible Agents AI driven CRM and the Rowdy Realtor Nation.

I call myself the Rowdy Realtor because Rowdy is my nickname and I was once a radio DJ and my radio name was Rowdy Tijmes (pronounced Times). I also built a concert company with my claim to fame being that I put Johnny Cash's band back together after he passed and put on a reunion show called the Johnny Cash Bash around the country. I have always had a passion for real estate, and have been a Realtor since 2017. I have ridden through the highs and lows of the different markets, becoming the top agent in Texas at one of the biggest brokerages. That wasn't luck. It was the result of building systems that work, staying ahead of the game, being a relentless negotiator, and using the latest technology, like AI, to keep me one step ahead and now I want to help you achieve your goals!

We're not just going to gloss over the tough parts. We'll dive into the real challenges that come with building a real estate business. You'll have the clarity and tools to create something that lasts once you cut through the distractions and tackle what's holding you back.

The truth is, you don't have to be the most intelligent person in the room to succeed. You just need the right mindset, the suitable systems, and a commitment to put in the work. If you can do that, you can build a business that stands the test of time—one that keeps growing long after you've moved on to the next chapter of your life.

This isn't about quick wins or shortcuts to get you to the top. It's about creating a real estate career that works for you, not the other way around. Ready to be a Future Proof Realtor? Let's get started.

CHAPTER 1:

NAVIGATING A SHIFTING MARKET - HOW TO FUTURE-PROOF YOURSELF IN SHIFTING MARKET CONDITIONS

To begin the book, let's talk about how to Future-Proof yourself before jumping into the AI side of things. Being that real estate is such a relationship business, it would be best to go over this information before diving deep as I am a firm believer that even though AI is a great tool, it is not the only tool that will make you stand out. The real estate world is unpredictable. If you've been in the game long enough, you know that markets can shift faster than a weather vane in a hurricane. One minute, you're in a seller's paradise, and the next, you're in a buyer's playground. If you don't know how to keep up, you're out of the game before even realizing it has changed.

My Shifting Market Story

I've been in real estate since 2017, and let me tell you, I've seen a lot! When I started, the market was uneventful, homes weren't flying off the shelves, and I had to hustle for every deal. Although, I did see that buyers were coming out more and more over the months as rates were dropping a little here and there. It felt like a completely different time, even though it wasn't all that long ago. It was a different time, back when every move wasn't instantly blasted across social media the moment news broke. But I saw what was happening, and I slowly set myself up for success. Then came the Covid-19 pandemic—a curveball no one saw coming. I had ten transactions in escrow, and I was feeling on top of the world. Then, in what felt like a blink of an eye, all my transactions fell apart. Every. Single. One.

People were scared, unsure of what the future held. Everyone was hitting the brakes, and suddenly, I was staring at a big fat zero on my closing sheet. It was one of those "oh crap" moments. What do you do when everything you've been working for evaporates overnight?

I adapted quickly. In a shifting market, the only way to not just survive, but thrive, is to stay flexible and pivot your strategy to meet the market head-on. That's exactly what I did. I assessed my options and made a tough but strategic choice. At the time, a new platform was offering the potential to reach new buyers and pay at closing. I also boldly switched brokerages—a tough decision since I loved where I was, but I needed to be part of the next big opportunity. I aligned myself with like-minded agents, and we dominated with referrals and leads. I also started learning the power of what was in my pocket, my cell phone. I helped numerous Buyers and Sellers purchase homes at that time without ever meeting them face to face but over Zoom. This is when my mind really started shifting and gave me a giant "Ah-Ha moment." I thought to myself, If I can sell homes without meeting people, what else can I do differently?

Fast forward to today, and we're in the middle of another shift, this time leaning towards buyers in many regions. The game has changed, but the fundamentals haven't. You must know who your clients are, what they want, and where to find them.

The System: Understanding Market Dynamics

The first step in navigating any shifting market is understanding what kind of market you're in. Are we dealing with a buyer's market or a seller's market? And more importantly, what are buyers or sellers looking for right now? Is it new construction? Is it homes on larger lots, is it more suburbs, is it inner city, is it a reasonable interest rate, what is it that most people are looking for, and how do I get in front of them?

As I am writing this, for example, new construction is a hot commodity. Buyers are looking for pristine, move-in-ready homes, and they're looking for lower interest rates (something you can negotiate with New Construction Builders).

Let's not beat around the bush, homes are expensive and just like everything else, they have jumped up in price. Buyers are unwilling to move into a house they just paid top dollar for and immediately have to start fixing it up (a little different than 2017). They don't want to deal with fixer-uppers or renovations—they want the Instagram-ready, picture-perfect home. So, what does that mean for you? It means you need to adjust your strategy. You need to shift your advertising to focus on what these buyers want. Target your marketing towards new construction or fully renovated properties. Use language that resonates with what they're looking for. My done for you advertising and marketing strategy at Accessible Agents does exactly this.

The key here is to always be one step ahead. You have to see where the market is going, not just where it is. This isn't rocket science; it's common sense combined with a bit of data and a lot of listening to what people are saying. Listen to what your clients are telling you, and if multiple people are saying the same thing, then you have proof of what people want.

And one other note I feel like I should add. If you're not getting out to these New Construction sites and simply talking to the sales reps and walking through their homes, you need to start doing that ASAP. I have gained so much knowledge from simply talking to the sales reps. Why? Because they literally have buyers walking into their offices just talking away and spilling all the beans. Pick those beans up and eat 'em! I just came up with that. But yes, pick up the dropped knowledge and use that to your advantage.

PRO TIP: Go to these new build sites on off days like Tuesday or Wednesday. They are not as busy those days and you can have more meaningful conversations with them. Be cool. Be nice. Offer to work with them. Give them your business card and be honest as to why you're there. You won't believe how much they'll open up to you. And you can use this information in your new AI campaign we'll be talking about later in the book in order to bring them customers and sell their homes.

Shifting Your Strategy

The beauty of real estate is that there are always buyers and sellers. The trick is figuring out who they are and how to get in front of them. During the pandemic, I learned this the hard way. I had to shift my strategy on the fly, and I discovered that even when it feels like the world is ending, people still need homes. They still need to buy, they still need to sell, and they're still out there—you just have to know where to look. In a shifting market, you have to be nimble. Your marketing has to be adaptable. Think of yourself as an investigator for a week and pick people's brains. Then use that information to your advantage. If you're still using the same tactics that worked last year, you're already behind. You need to know where the demand is and position yourself right in front of it.

The Takeaway

At the end of the day, a shifting market isn't something to be afraid of. It's an opportunity. It should be exciting! It's a chance to stand out while everyone else is scrambling. It's your time to step up and lead. While others are stuck in their old ways, you'll be the one adapting, evolving, and thriving. It can be a little scary at first but once your new strategy starts working, it's a breath of fresh air. And that's one huge way you future-proof your career in a shifting market.

CHAPTER 2:

MOVING AROUND– DOMINATING ANY MARKET WITH THE RIGHT STRATEGY

Real estate agents are often creatures of habit. They find a market they're comfortable in, set up shop, and plant roots. And why not? It's tough enough to build a name for yourself without uprooting everything and starting from scratch somewhere else. But what if I told you that with the proper marketing and mindset, you could succeed in any market, anywhere? And in not too much time? Sounds crazy? Well, let me share my story.

From Oregon to Texas: My Journey of Reinvention

I began my real estate career in Oregon, navigating the lush landscapes and unique challenges of the Pacific Northwest. I started in Portland and then expanded into Washington State, which required me to get an additional license. After six years of building my business, life threw me a curveball. Having been originally from Texas, I felt it was best to move back and be closer to my family and my dear old friends. So, I made the big decision to pack up and head back to Houston.

Now, this wasn't just a move across town. It was a complete market shift, from the rainy, laid-back scenes of Portland to the fast-paced sprawling cityscape of the fourth-largest city in the country. This meant that I was again starting from scratch—zero clients, zero reputation, and not too much market knowledge except for what my family was telling me about what was going on in their tiny pocket. They weren't even in real estate, so I took it all with a grain of salt. I had to rebuild my business from the ground up. But again, I had a strategy, and after only one and a half years in Texas, I was named the top #1 realtor in Texas by volume for three different months at eXp Realty. I was named #2 in the country by volume at eXp Realty with around 90,000 agents. And I was number 149 for the year, out of approximately 90,000 agents at eXp Realty. I honestly still can't believe it. I didn't even do that while in Oregon.

And it was not because I had a leg up over anyone else. I will say that I did get my Texas license BEFORE moving to Texas and I started out by flying back and forth and helping clients in both states for about 6 months before I ultimately moved. There's something amazing about technology. I'll give you another little secret. You don't have to be somewhere anymore to start advertising, marketing, or even showing homes. You can do it from your phone anywhere in the world.

Most realtors I spoke to said I was crazy for wanting to move after building such a reputable name for myself the last 5 years and working so hard to build what I built. Why move? Why not get bigger here? My answer to them: If I can do it here, I can do it anywhere. And Houston being the 4th largest city in the country, if I can't make a living being surrounded by 8 Million people, then where could I make a living? Moving to a new city means leaving behind all your hard-earned connections, your local market expertise, your reputation, and your comfort zone. But here's the thing: I wasn't afraid. I had a plan. What's that famous saying by good ol' Benjamin Franklin? "If you fail to plan, you're planning to fail."

The Power of the Right Marketing

You see, I wasn't just relying on luck or hoping to catch a break. I had developed a marketing system that I knew would work, no matter where I went. With this system,

I was able to analyze the local market, identify potential clients, and position myself right in front of them.

I also had to make another big decision that I wasn't ready for. Life throws curveballs all the time, and you need to know this is going to happen. Do not be afraid of it, simply embrace it and ride the wave. The next big decision I didn't anticipate was finding a new brokerage—again. I liked my place in Portland, and I built many lasting relationships that I still maintain today. Leaving wasn't something I wanted, and I certainly didn't want to leave on bad terms. But what I hadn't realized was that staying would mean paying two separate cap rates at two brick-and-mortar brokerages. I'd already seen colleagues at eXp making waves in the industry, so I began asking why they were suddenly so much more successful. What I learned was game-changing—there were no boundaries with a cloud-based brokerage. I could work across multiple states, hold multiple licenses, and only pay one cap rate. If I stayed, I'd be stuck with multiple fees, and my Texas license would have violated a non-compete clause. That realization made it clear: eXp's cloud-based model was the future, and after looking into it, I was even more impressed. I'll share more on that later.

Within a year and a half of moving to Houston, I became the number one agent by volume in Texas at my brokerage, eXp Realty. That's right—no previous clients, no big connections, not even previous work history there (I left right after high school), just the right strategy and a lot of hustle.

The lesson here? Realtors (or entrepreneurs in general) shouldn't fear moving to a new city, state, or even a different MLS area. With the proper marketing techniques in place, you won't just survive—you'll thrive. Sure, you might be starting from zero, but zero is just a number and who knows you're new to the area unless you tell them. People will see your drive, determination, and knowledge and they won't question you if you provide a great service. What matters is your ability to adapt, learn, and implement strategies that work. You have to be confident.

Why Realtors Fear Moving (or Starting From Scratch)

The idea of starting over can be terrifying. It's not just about learning the local market; it's about building a whole new network, creating new relationships, and establishing yourself in a community that doesn't know you. Most agents think, "What if I can't find new clients? What if I don't fit in? What if I fail miserably? What if? What if? What if?" The What-ifs are endless.

They are valid concerns, but they're rooted in fear. Fear of the unknown, fear of failure, and fear of losing what you've built. But here's the reality: fear is just a mental roadblock. And if you can't get over mental roadblocks, how will you elevate your career? With the right mindset, the right guidance, and the proper marketing, you can break through any barrier. You can dominate any market, no matter where you are. I'm living proof of that. I've done it, and so can you!

The Secret Sauce: Proven Marketing Methods

So, what's the secret? What did I do differently? How do you go from zero to hero in a completely new market? It all comes down to having a robust marketing plan that's adaptable to any environment. Here's a glimpse of what worked for me (and will work for you even if you're not considering moving):

Market Research: Know the Lay of the Land

Before you start advertising, The most critical step is understanding the market. This goes beyond just knowing the average home price. You need to have a deep understanding of who your target buyers and sellers are. What type of properties are they interested in? Are families with children moving to the area for good schools, or is it a hotspot for young professionals? This goes back to when I suggested taking a week to become an investigator. That one week will catapult you over all the competition.

Dive Deep into local market trends. Are there areas experiencing growth or gentrification? Analyze how many listings are on the market and figure out what makes them appealing. Where are the hot spots? Why are they hot? This information is sitting right there in your MLS if you know where to look. Your goal is to gather as much data as possible to avoid walking in blind. The more you understand the nuances of the market, the better you'll be able to position yourself as the go-to agent.

Here's another Pro-Tip: USE AI to save yourself a whole bunch of time researching! Ask AI what areas have the least amount of Days On the Market. Ask AI where the best schools are. Ask AI what area has the highest and lowest price per sq ft. Ask AI what builders are the least expensive. Ask AI what types of homes are in a certain area. Ask AI where developers and builders are purchasing land. You can even ask AI where people are moving from most or what is the most common reason people are moving to XYZ city. Ask AI where companies are moving to/from. In about 10 minutes, I can get so much information and all of this information is going to determine how and where I'll be advertising. More information on my advertising methods later in the book.

Brand Positioning: Become the Expert
You can't just show up and hope people will come to you. You have to make people believe you're the expert, even if you're brand new to the area. This starts by creating valuable content that speaks directly to the needs of

your local audience. But here's the thing—people don't want to be bombarded with raw data. They want to know how this information applies to them and their dream of buying or selling a home.

Yes, share insights, market trends, and valuable stats, but wrap them in storytelling that adds personality and relevance. When you speak to your audience in a way that resonates with their desires, you're not just giving them data, you're selling them a dream. Be mindful of your delivery—nobody wants a dry data dump. They want excitement, vision, and a path to a future home.

When you find that balance between information and inspiration, you'll hook your audience right in! Then what? Then when you see them engaged with what you're saying, you ask for their information and tell them you have an awesome weekly newsletter and you'd love to send it to them. BAM! You now have a future client. And how did you get them? By simply asking AI important questions about the area and by being you and adding that added extra personal spice. POW!

Do this over and over again to the people you meet at the gym, grocery store, kids' school, pool, walking your dog, etc... and I guarantee you that you'll get clients.

Digital Presence: Your Online Lifeline

In a world where everyone's first instinct is to Google you, your digital presence is your lifeline. If someone searches your name or your listings and can't find you, you've already lost. Start with a professional, easy-to-navigate website that showcases your listings, provides valuable insights, and has a clear call to action. Then, optimize your site for local SEO so potential clients can find you through relevant search terms.

Don't forget about social media. Make sure your profiles are up-to-date and that you're engaging with your audience regularly. This is where you can build a personal brand that people trust. Use social media to show off beautiful homes, share market tips, and engage in local community groups to make yourself known. And if you're in a new market, targeted digital ads are a great way to get your name in front of the right people. Consistent, strategic posting keeps you top of mind when potential clients are ready to make a move. When you ask for people's information, make sure to ask about their social media pages too. My Accessible Agents CRM I created does all of this for you in one place.

Networking: Get Out and Make Connections :

Join local organizations, attend community events, and be active in the places where your potential clients are spending their time. Real estate is a relationship business, and people are more likely to trust and work with someone they've met in person.

But here's the kicker—this isn't a one-and-done strategy. You need to be consistent. Showing up once won't leave a lasting impression. You need to be present, introduce yourself, and continually build relationships. Hand out business cards, shake hands, and make sure people associate your name with real estate in their area. The more often they see your face, the more likely they are to remember you when they need to buy or sell a home.

I know this sounds like a lot but just pick one. Pick something. It doesn't have to be go go go always attending events. It can just be one thing that you're passionate about. Maybe it's cars; go to car shows. Maybe it's art; attend local arts events. Maybe it's quilting; attend a monthly quilting group.

But Martin: I thought this was about AI and not going into the community. Remember: AI is here to help us. Not replace us. Anyone can use AI but not everyone does. And why don't people buy homes from AI or robots (it has been attempted and failed miserably)? It's because this is a relationship business. Keep asking AI questions (that take 1 minute to do) and simply add your own personality when you're talking to people and you sound like a local expert people can trust.

Follow-Up System: Stay on Their Radar
I might mention this a few more times but you need to be able to consistently follow up. Once you've made those initial connections, the real work begins. The key to converting leads into clients is consistent follow-up. Whether it's through email, phone calls, or texts, you need a solid system in place to nurture your leads. The best agents aren't the ones who send one email and forget about it—they're the ones who maintain ongoing relationships with their leads.

Set reminders, follow up regularly, and provide value with every touchpoint. You don't want to come across as pushy, but you do want to stay top of mind. Maybe it's a market update, maybe it's a personalized note on a recent neighborhood sale—whatever it is, make sure it's relevant and useful to your leads. The more you can show that you're actively engaged in their real estate journey, the more likely they are to call you when they're ready to make a move. I was having such a hard time doing all this I thought there should be a better way and there is! My Accessible Agents CRM with AI technology does all of this for you.

The Takeaway
Realtors shouldn't let fear hold them back from pursuing new opportunities. Moving to a new market isn't easy, but it's not impossible. With the right marketing strategy and

a good work ethic, you can succeed anywhere. Remember, it's not about where you start—it's about where you're willing to go, reaching your highest potential. If I can move from Oregon to Texas and become the top agent in a year and a half, there's no reason you can't.

How does this pertain to Future-Proofing yourself as a Realtor? Be strategic in what you do. With the right marketing and data, you can succeed and thrive.

CHAPTER 3:

THE REMOTE REALTOR

If you had told me a few years ago that I could sell a house without ever setting foot in it, I would have laughed you out of the room. The idea of closing a deal without shaking hands or walking through the property seemed impossible. It didn't even seem impossible, I couldn't even imagine it. But here we are, and not only is it possible—it's becoming the norm. I've sold homes from 2,500 miles away without ever meeting the buyer, the seller, or even stepping inside the house. And I'm not just talking about a one-time deal—I do this all the time now. I know you're thinking "What?! How?! Aren't you providing bad service for your clients?! What are you talking about?!" Yeah, I get those questions all the time and lucky for you, I'm about to spill the beans. So pick them up!

The Remote Real Estate Revolution

Back in the day, selling a house meant being there in person for every step of the process. You had to meet the clients, show the property, host open houses, be at the inspection, be at the closing table, and be everywhere. But things have changed. With the rise of technology and the push towards virtual interactions (thanks to COVID-19), the real estate world has gone through a major transformation. You no longer need to be physically present to close deals. I've successfully managed transactions from thousands of miles away, all thanks to the digital tools and strategies that are at our everyday disposal! You just need to know how to use them. And be confident!

Let me give you an example. I started my real estate career in Oregon, but after a few years, I decided to move back to my hometown of Houston, Texas. Even though I was now based in a completely different state with a completely different mindset, I still had clients and properties in Oregon. I was mentally having issues with helping clients in a different state, so I was flying back and forth a lot. I had a rental property in Oregon and I thought, "Let me try this out on myself before I try it on a client." I decided to put my own home on the market to see if I could sell it without going back. And guess what? I did it! Not only did I do it, but I did it in a buyer's market where it was difficult to sell a home and I never flew back to the property during any part of the sales process. I wanted to multiple times but I made myself figure it out. Was it risky? Heck yeah!! I had never done this before. But, I needed to know if I could do it and I was confident I could.

From 2,500 miles away, I coordinated everything—the photography, the showings, the open houses, the marketing, and even the closing—all without ever stepping foot in the house. I did not fly back until I was 100% closed and only needed to go back in order to move. And honestly, I probably could've done that remotely too. I hired people to be my eyes and ears on the ground. I used Zoom for client meetings, and I managed the entire transaction from start to finish 2,500 miles away. It was a seamless process, and it showed me that distance is no longer a barrier in real estate! I was honestly taken aback by what could be accomplished from so far away.

The Power of Technology

The secret to selling real estate remotely is using the right technology. I work with eXp Realty, a cloud-based brokerage that offers a virtual office space. It's like something out of a video game—I have an avatar, and I can literally walk into my digital office, talk to my principal brokers, and access all the resources I need as if I were there in person. This level of accessibility is a game-changer, especially when you're managing transactions from different states or simply just want to save a lot of time. I can be anywhere in the world and "walk in" to my office and ask my managing broker any question I want. It's awesome!

Zoom has also become my best friend. I use it for everything—from initial consultations to virtual property tours to closing meetings. Guess what? My clients love it too! At first, it was a mental block that my clients wouldn't like it. But I never tried! Mental roadblock. Now, I'm saving time by not driving to meet them somewhere and we do the meeting and get to business. They also like it! Of course, I do like human interaction so I definitely meet people too.

I also hire local buyer agents to be my boots on the ground. They view properties for my clients, conduct inspections, and provide real-time feedback. And I can virtually walk through the properties and see what they see! This way, I'm not just relying on my own eyes—I have a team of experts providing input. In many ways, I'm offering my clients more value because I have multiple people looking at the property from different perspectives than just myself.

How to Sell Remotely: The Blueprint

So, how can you successfully sell real estate in another state while living thousands of miles away? Or even another way to ask the question: how can you successfully sell more real estate by saving time? Here's the step-by-step blueprint:

Establish a Reliable Local Team (and no, I am not talking about people you need to physically manage)

You need trustworthy people on the ground—buyer agents, photographers, inspectors—who can act as your eyes and ears. These individuals should be experts in their own right, capable of handling the physical aspects of the transaction with little oversight. They're the ones who will handle the physical aspects of the transaction while you manage the rest remotely. The key here is to trust them to do their job so you can focus on the bigger picture.

Leverage Virtual Tools

In today's digital world, distance is thankfully no longer a barrier. Zoom, virtual tours, and e-signatures are your new best friends. Use them to conduct meetings, show properties, and sign documents. Use video conferencing for meetings and consultations. Virtual tours to show homes and anything that can be automated to keep things moving. The more comfortable you are with these tools, the more seamless your transactions will be. This shows clients that you are available to them from anywhere and also proactive in making their experience seamless, even from miles away. It's all about creating that personal connection without the need to be there physically.

Communicate Clearly and Consistently

When working remotely, communication becomes your greatest ally. Set expectations upfront with both your clients and your local team—clarity is key. Make sure your clients understand exactly what the process will look like, who they'll be meeting, and when they can expect updates. This prevents any possible misunderstandings and builds trust. Being upfront about not physically attending every showing gives you more credibility—clients will appreciate the transparency and view you as someone who's managing multiple deals, not just focused on theirs. The more you communicate, the more in control you seem, even from afar.

Use a Cloud-Based Brokerage

If your brokerage isn't leveraging modern technology, you're missing out on a huge advantage. Cloud-based brokerages, like eXp Realty, offer virtual offices, instant access to brokers, and a suite of digital resources that make remote work not only possible but seamless. Imagine being able to walk into your brokerage's office without actually being there. With a cloud-based system, you can stay in touch with your brokerage and manage deals from anywhere. This gives you the freedom to work across states without juggling physical office space or location-based limitations. I am hiring so please feel free to reach out with any questions about the brokerage. My contact info is on the back cover.

Stay Organized

Managing multiple transactions can be overwhelming if you are not organized. A sturdy CRM system is your lifeline here. Use it to track contracts, schedule follow-ups and keep all your deadlines in check. Anything from sending out reminders to managing listings, a CRM will ensure you never drop your hat, no matter how many deals you're juggling across different locations. This level of organization will set you apart from others who rely on manual tracking and outdated Excel sheets. Staying organized and being efficient is the name of the game. I actually created a very robust one for agents like you to succeed. Being an agent, I know what you need so I created the ultimate CRM with AI installed!

Be Ready to Be There in Person If Needed

While most transactions can be handled remotely, there are times when showing up in person is necessary. That said, be selective. Don't waste time driving or flying out for deals that aren't likely to close or that don't require your direct involvement. Remember, we're not doctors. In real estate, very few things are urgent enough to justify being there in person. But, when a deal is nearing the finish line and it needs that personal touch, being there in person can make all the difference.

The Future of Real Estate is Remote

If Covid taught us anything, it's that we need to be adaptable. The real estate industry has been forced to innovate, and remote transactions are now more common than ever. But it's not just a response to the pandemic—it's the future. Buyers and sellers are getting more comfortable with the idea of virtual transactions, and as agents, we need to meet their standards and that doesn't technically mean meeting them in person.

The ability to sell homes from anywhere gives you a massive advantage. You have way more time on your hands, you're not tied down to one market, and you can continue to serve your clients even if you decide to move. It's all about having the right systems in place and being willing to embrace the tools available to you. By implementing these systems, you can have financial, time and location freedom.

The Takeaway

Selling real estate remotely isn't just possible—it's efficient, effective, and often more convenient for both you and your clients. With the right approach, you can manage transactions from any corner of the world, provide exceptional service, and continue to grow your business no matter where you are. It's time to stop thinking of distance as a barrier and start seeing it as an opportunity.

The miles don't matter, but the strategy does. If I can do it from 2500 miles away, you can too.

How is this Future Proofing your Business?

This strategy can be used anywhere. It does not mean that you have to move for it in order to work. You can be 1 mile away from your next appointment and still use this strategy. It frees up a lot of time from driving and meeting people in person. And don't get me wrong, I love people. I love interacting with people and I love helping them. Sometimes I do meet with people face to face and that's totally fine. This method frees up a lot of time for you to work on getting more clients and moving the needle rather than driving all around town in an endless commute. This is one big way in which I was able to gain more clients and become a top producer. I integrated all of these tools into my Accessible Agents CRM. And Rowdy Realtor Nation is the online community where one can converse with other Realtors and hear what people are doing to take their business to the next level.

CHAPTER 4:

FUTURE PROOF YOUR CAREER BY NOT BEING A SUCKY AGENT

Let's just be blunt—real estate is filled with bad, sucky agents. Yep, I said it. And if you've done any number of transactions, you know what I mean. The ones who slap a listing up on MLS with the wrong info, fail to verify anything, use awful photos, and think yelling at you is a great way to negotiate. It's like they're actively doing everything possible to *not* sell a house and give the rest of us a bad name.

Agents need coaching and I want to show you **how not to be that agent**. If you want to future-proof your career and stand out in this industry, the first step is simple: **Don't suck**! Honestly, this applies to any industry or job. Want a promotion? Learn, be open-minded, and get your clients what they want. In real estate, a promotion is word of mouth, and more transactions are needed to show for it.

What Makes a Bad Agent?

If I had to sum it up, a bad agent is someone who doesn't **utilize their resources and is closed-minded**. They refuse to take the action that is needed and grow. It's as if they're working in isolation, ignoring all the help their brokerage provides, and making rookie mistakes left and right because they don't want to learn and think their way is the best. Like mislisting square footage or forgetting key details in contracts. And don't get me started on the yelling to get their way. These are the cardinal signs of real estate that can make deals fall apart.

Let me tell you about one such agent I worked with. I was the Buyer's agent, and the Listing Agent didn't bother verifying anything. The rent listed was wrong (I had to verify by asking multiple times for the lease agreement), the square footage was off (I verified this by county records and the appraiser), and when I confronted the agent, they tried to pass the blame to their principal broker and the photographer. The photographer is now giving square footage details. So strange and unprofessional! Better yet, I even received a screenshot written to the listing agent by the county describing the square footage but the listing agent wanted to put a bigger number on the MLS, so they did. Then we almost got out of contract because the price was too high for the "real" square footage and I told my Buyers that it's a gamble but I think we should get the house appraised. It's a gamble because the Buyers had to pay for it. Thankfully I had clients that listened to me and we did go ahead with the appraisal. Sure enough, it was listed wrong and I negotiated nearly 10% off and came out looking like a hero. Now who do you think they're going to refer to their friends and colleagues in the future? Let me be clear: **If you're blaming your principal broker or anyone else for your mistakes, you're doing it all wrong.** I understand our job is to get the best for our clients, but using false information, throwing blame, or trying to strong-arm people is far from a winning negotiation strategy. It does the opposite—it alienates people and causes deals to fall apart. Somehow, I managed to keep this deal on track, despite it nearly collapsing multiple times. And why did it almost collapse multiple times? Because the listing agent was simply being a sucky agent. They were acting like it was their house. Look, being a Realtor is a job. Be professional and don't yell at your fellow Realtors. That negotiation strategy is a deal killer. We're all here for the same outcome: to sell the property.

The kicker? They weren't even using their broker as a resource! That's literally what they're there for—to answer questions, help navigate tricky transactions, and make sure agents aren't out there making fools of themselves. If you're paying your brokerage fees and **not** utilizing their resources, you're wasting both your money and your career. Not to mention making a bad name not only for yourself but also for your brokerage.

I've seen this more times than I can count, and I'm sure you have too. One time, I was the listing agent, and the buyer's agent kept obsessing over commission—constantly asking about it, even though they were already making a hefty sum from the transaction. The strangest part? When it came time for amendments or anything technical, they were completely lost and asked *me* to handle it and write it all up for their clients! I couldn't believe it. They were making my job harder while adding no value. I started thinking, *Why are we even paying them a commission at all?* They clearly lacked mentorship—or maybe they never had one in the first place. This agent could've used AI to help in creating the right documents. I'm going to say it again: Use your resources! AI is here to help us!

Step One: Use Your Resources

Look, your principal broker is there to help. If you have questions, ask them. Do not ask a forum, or your friend that sold a house once. Ask people who are working in real estate full-time. If you're not sure about the details of a property, dig deeper. Use the public records, look up county records, call the title company, ask your broker, whatever you need to do. Just **don't wing it**. We are SELLING REAL ESTATE! The BIGGEST INVESTMENT! Not only that, but it is also the BIGGEST thing someone physically owns.

Pro Tip: You can ask AI anything about a particular house and this will also save you time to dig deeper the old-fashioned way like I just described.

Imagine working at a Lamborghini dealership. Would you guess on engine specs, give clients the wrong horsepower, or yell at them when they ask for details? Of course not! That would not only cost you the sale but you'll drive all business away, get a bad rep, and get fired. In today's world, we have access to an abundance of information—there's no reason not to use it. Whether it's verifying property details or answering client questions, doing your due diligence shows professionalism and earns trust.

Here's a reality check: If you're going to slap something up on MLS, make sure it's accurate. Verify the square footage, confirm factual information, and for heaven's sake, don't just rely on what the seller told you. Cross-check everything because you're not just protecting your client—you're protecting your reputation. This does take a little time upfront but I guarantee you the extra 10 minutes will save you multiple hours and headaches later on when you're in contract. And then you'll most likely get out of the contract because of wrong information and upset buyers or sellers.

I pride myself on being one of the best at keeping transactions together. I've had several clients ready to walk away from deals, but I managed to hold things together—not through emotion, but by relying on facts and practical solutions. Now, I'm not saying you should force clients to stay in a deal if they truly want out, but most times, they're backing out because of solvable concerns. They liked the property enough to get this far, so it's our job to figure out what's causing the hesitation and address it. That's what we get paid to do. It's not easy, but it's not rocket science either.

The key? Keep emotions out of it. Make decisions based on facts, not feelings. Ask questions, get to the root of the issue, and then use the resources at your disposal to find a solution. When you approach it this way, you're not just keeping deals together—you're proving your value as a trusted advisor and problem solver.

STEP TWO: DON'T LIE

Honesty should be a given, but in real estate, I've seen agents bend the truth more than a yoga instructor. Lying, whether about a property's condition, age of items on the property, rental history, or even pointing fingers that can easily be worked out, is a fast way to lose your license and your credibility. Did you know that you can use AI to tell you the age of appliances and items on the property? Another huge time saver!!

A bad agent might think they can fudge the details and get away with it, but the truth always comes out. Just like in the case of that duplex, where I had to spend hours fixing the mess the listing agent created because they weren't being upfront. Don't be that agent! THIS IS YOUR JOB! THIS IS NOT YOUR PROPERTY! **Be transparent, be honest, and double-check everything** before you hit "submit." Better yet, have AI double-check it for you. Another time saver!!

Step Three: Understand the Transaction

The real key to being a great agent? Understand the mechanics of the transaction. It's not just about showing houses—it's about guiding your clients through one of the most significant financial decisions they'll ever make. The real work begins after the property is found and the contract is written. Yet, there's this common misconception: "All you do is open doors and cash checks." If that were true, everyone would be millionaires overnight, and the failure rate in real estate wouldn't be hovering around 90%. Finding the property is the easy part. Navigating the sale is a whole different story.

Take the transaction I just mentioned for example. My clients were ready to back out because of the price and the square footage issue. Most agents would've just terminated the contract and started looking again. But here's the truth: that's the lazy route and it actually wastes more time. Why walk away when you could renegotiate and save the deal? Instead of abandoning the ship, I sat down with them to figure out the real issue: they loved the house and the area—what they didn't like was the price. That's where negotiation comes in.

I knew the appraisal hadn't been done yet, so I suggested we roll the dice. Based on my research, I had a good feeling the property wouldn't appraise at the asking price. Sure enough, it came in lower because the listing agent had input the wrong square footage, which ended up saving my clients almost 10% on a property valued at over half a million dollars. If I had walked away, my clients would've lost their dream homes, and I'd have wasted all the work I put in. Instead, I helped them secure the house they loved, saved them a significant amount, and proved my value in the process. I didn't just close a deal—I earned their trust for life.

I came out the hero and proved my worth by an incredible amount. I Future-Proofed my career with these clients.

Step Four: Referrals and Repeat Clients

Speaking of referrals, people will talk about their large real estate purchases and who helped them. Give them something to talk about! They'll tell their friends, family, and co-workers about you. My Buyers I've been talking about? They were **repeat clients** because I had done a good job for them the first time around. This business isn't just about closing one deal, it's about building relationships that lead to future business. And guess what? I also helped them from 2500 miles away!

If you take care of your clients, they'll take care of you. **Referrals are gold** in this industry, and if you're doing the job right, you'll get plenty of them. But here's the catch: You have to deliver consistently excellent service. No one's going to recommend an agent who cuts corners or didn't fight for them.

Step Five: Keep Learning (But Don't Get Distracted)

Lastly, stay educated, but don't fall into the trap of **chasing every shiny object**. It's easy to get caught up in the latest course or marketing tactic that promises to make you a million dollars overnight. But the truth is, most agents spend more time chasing the new shiny object than actually working. It's great to keep your skills sharp and know what's out there, but don't use these shiny new objects as an excuse for inaction.

Real estate is a hands-on business, and the more you **do the work**, the more successful you'll be. So yes, take the courses, and go to the seminars, but remember: **learning without action is useless**.

The Takeaway

At the end of the day, **don't be a sucky agent**. Be the agent who uses their resources, communicates, verifies everything, and goes above and beyond for their clients. That's how you future-proof your career. That's how you get referrals, and that's how you succeed in this business without burning out. It's a fun job when you close on a tough transaction and help your clients do something they could not have done on their own! But that's where you can show off your skills, get people what they want, and walk away as a forever hero to a client for life. With my Accessible Agents CRM, I also offer coaching along with other top producing agents. Check it out at AccessibleAgents.com

CHAPTER 5:

THE GRASS IS GREENER WHERE YOU WATER IT

Throughout my career, I've worked at five different brokerages. Five. Every time I made a move, I had what seemed like solid reasons—lack of support, commission splits too steep, or a culture that just didn't click. I kept chasing the "perfect" brokerage, thinking the grass had to be greener somewhere else. Spoiler alert: it wasn't. But here's what I discovered along the way—each stop taught me valuable lessons, and after all that searching, I finally found where I truly belong.

You see, like a lot of realtors, I fell victim to **shiny object syndrome**. There are so many "gurus" out there, and as independent contractors, we're constantly bombarded with high-ticket offers from new brokerages or systems that promise to make us rich. It's easy to get lured in, thinking, "If I just switch to this brokerage, everything will be better." But the truth is, **the grass is greener where you water it**.

The Temptation to Jump

I'll admit, I've jumped around. My first brokerage was a small, boutique firm. I thought, "Smaller means more personalized support, right?" Wrong. My principal broker had many different businesses and was never available. I remember one day, I had a critical question that needed an answer before 5 p.m., and when I approached my broker, he was running out the door for a haircut appointment, wouldn't stop to answer my question, and no one else was around to answer my question. I was left hanging as a brand new agent and was clueless about how to resolve my client's issue.

That was the moment I realized I needed to find a better place. A place that has access to a broker when I have an issue arise. I switched to a larger, franchise brokerage, thinking bigger meant better training and more resources. While they had great training, it was hours of how to read a contract—stuff I could have learned on my own in half the time. And their commission splits? **Astronomically high.** I'd close a deal and barely see the money after all their fees.

One day, I went into the office and spoke to my broker all excited and said, "Hey! I'm going to start knocking on doors in XYZ neighborhood. I can't wait to talk to everyone there!" My broker immediately said, **"Don't waste your time there. Everyone already has a Realtor in that neighborhood."** I felt deflated. I thought she would be happy for me and give me advice. Nope. But that statement felt like a dare to me. So I ignored her advice, knocked on those doors, and guess what? I found a buyer! A GREAT buyer!! And I so badly needed that sale as I hadn't closed anything in months due to a mountain biking wreck I was in. That sale should have been a win—until I saw my paycheck. Out of $18,000, I walked away with a little over $10,000. The brokerage took $8,000 for doing what? Telling me not to bother with door knocking in the area I wanted to door knock on? And the brokerage did nothing during the transaction. And I was not learning anything new like they promised. That's when I knew I had to leave.

Finding Good Dirt

The lesson here? **The grass is green where you water it, but you need GOOD DIRT!** You can work as hard as you want, but if you're not in the right environment with fertile soil, your efforts will be wasted. After bouncing from brokerage to brokerage, I finally found my home at eXp Realty. And you know what the difference is? **Support. FAST SUPPORT and A LOT OF TRAINING and UNCONVENTIONAL THINKING.**

At eXp, I don't have to chase down my principal broker or worry about missed questions. I can hop online, and get answers from one of the many brokers available in our virtual office. That's what I call "good dirt." It's the kind of support that allows me to grow, focus on my clients, and **water my grass**.

More "good dirt" is in the training. Unlike one of my past brokerages that told me not to door-knock on a specific neighborhood, eXp allows me to use tools that will ultimately get me more transactions! And they encourage thinking outside the box and helping agents grow their business.

One thing I do know, if I had been with eXp from the beginning, I would have gotten to this point much faster. My colleagues always ask me why? Are you sure? My answer is always a resounding YES—100%! If I had just done the exact same thing I was doing but just at this brokerage, I would've had more support, more ideas, fewer boundaries, more money, and a larger business.

The Power of Sticking with One Thing

In real estate and life, success doesn't come from constantly chasing the next big thing. It comes from **sticking with one thing** long enough to see it grow. I'm not saying you should stay at a brokerage that doesn't support you—if you're in bad dirt, you're not going to grow. But once you find a place that offers good support, good people, and the tools you need, **stick with it**.

The Good Brokerage: People, Support, Tools

So, what makes a good brokerage? In my experience, it comes down to the **three G's**:

1. **Great People:** The key here isn't just about having a mentor but having access to top producers—people who are not only at the peak of their careers but are also willing to share their strategies and insights with you. If your brokerage is filled with people who keep their success secrets to themselves or offer generic, surface-level advice, you're in the wrong place. Real training from high-level agents who push you to think outside the box is essential. You should be learning from those who have been where you are and who are willing to show you the ropes, even their so-called trade secrets. We are a team and I love seeing agents grow.

2. **Great Support:** Whether your brokerage is cloud-based or operates out of a traditional brick-and-mortar office, having strong, consistent support is non-negotiable. In this business, things move fast, and you can't afford to wait days or even hours for your broker to answer a

question. This is one of the reasons I'm with eXp Realty. I don't have to chase down one person who's always out of the office or bogged down with their own clients. I have access to multiple brokers who are available when I need them—whether it's to help with a complex transaction or clarify compliance issues. This kind of reliable, accessible support allows you to focus on what matters—your clients—while knowing you're backed by a strong, responsive team.

3. **Great Tools:** From AI lead generation to CRM systems, your brokerage should provide you with the tools to succeed in the modern real estate market. The modern real estate market isn't just about pounding the pavement and making cold calls. If your brokerage isn't offering you cutting-edge tools, you're already falling behind. Your brokerage should be equipping you with systems that help you manage leads, automate follow-ups, and streamline your workflow so that you can focus on closing deals—not spending hours chasing down leads manually. Time is your most valuable asset, and a great brokerage provides you with the technology to maximize it. From data analytics tools to AI-driven marketing, the right tools help you operate efficiently and effectively in a competitive industry. This is

exactly the reason why I have created my own CRM that has everything agents are looking for! And guess what? My brokerage completely supports my decision. As a top producer, I felt I needed a little more out of a CRM. So I decided to create one that has all the AI technology I've been talking about in this book and I offer this to my nationwide team for free. I simply want to see them do better and help them crush the real estate game.

The Temptation to Jump Continued

Even in the best environment, the temptation to jump will always be there. You'll hear about new brokerages offering better splits, or you'll get frustrated with a slow month and think about quitting. But remember this: **The grass is greener where you water it.** You've got to put in the work, even when it's hard. Those potential clients who may not be ready now, will be in the future. And if you've found the right place, stay there, plant your seeds and wait for them to keep growing. Bottom line: treat this job as if you are going to work every day and have a boss. Pretend there is a boss behind your back micromanaging you and watching you clock in. If you put in the work, you will succeed.

The Takeaway

The grass isn't greener on the other side. It's greener where you water it—and where you've planted yourself in **good dirt**. Find a brokerage with good people, solid support, and the right tools. Resist the urge to jump ship every time you hit a rough patch, and instead, focus on nurturing your business where you are. That's how you'll grow, make more money, and future-proof your career.

CHAPTER 6:

SELL HOMES SYSTEMATICALLY, DON'T BE THE COG

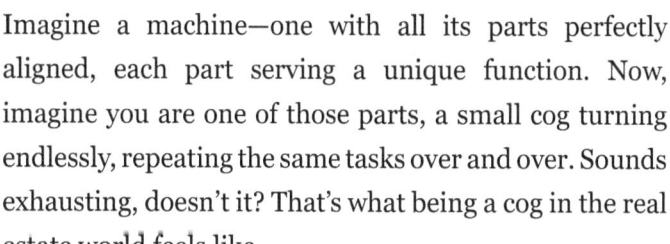

Imagine a machine—one with all its parts perfectly aligned, each part serving a unique function. Now, imagine you are one of those parts, a small cog turning endlessly, repeating the same tasks over and over. Sounds exhausting, doesn't it? That's what being a cog in the real estate world feels like.

Early in my career, I was that cog. I was running around, doing everything manually—prospecting, making cold calls, door-knocking, doing digital marketing, scheduling meetings, showing homes, chasing down paperwork, and trying to juggle it all. I was spinning so fast that I didn't even have time to think about whether

I was being effective. **And let me tell you, that's no way to run a business.**

The Reality of Being the Cog

In the real estate industry, you can easily fall into the trap of thinking that the more hours you work, the more successful you'll be. But that's a myth. Working harder doesn't mean you're working smarter. It often means the opposite. When you're constantly running from one task to another, trying to be everything to everyone, you're not growing. You're just doing more of the same and trying to survive and catch your breath. It can feel so overwhelming.

I was chasing leads by cold-calling and knocking on doors, hoping to stumble across a sale. I'd spend hours dialing number after number, following up on old contacts, sending endless emails, and setting up meetings—only to face cancellation after cancellation. If someone told me about a new marketing tactic, I'd jump on it, hoping it would be the magic solution to my overwhelm. But all I was doing was adding more tasks to my already overfilled plate.

I wasn't running my business; my business was running me.

Building a System

The turning point came when I realized I couldn't keep working like that. I needed a system—a **machine** that would take on the tasks I didn't need to personally do, so I could focus on what mattered: **closing deals**.

Selling homes systematically is not just about streamlining processes; it's about putting a structure in place that allows you to scale. This means creating a system that can operate independently of you, so you're no longer a cog. You're the conductor.

And let me be clear: This isn't just for big teams or agencies. Even as a solo agent, you can build a machine that works for you, rather than the other way around. That's where technology—particularly **AI** and **CRM systems**—comes in.

The Power of Technology

When I first started integrating AI and CRM systems into my business, it felt like I'd unlocked a cheat code. Suddenly, I had a tool that could handle the grunt work for me—sorting leads, following up, scheduling meetings, and even starting the conversation before I ever picked up the phone.

Let me walk you through it.

When a lead comes in, my Accessible Agents CRM automatically reaches out. A bot sends the initial message, introducing itself as my assistant. It doesn't feel robotic because I've spent months developing a personality for it. It's friendly, approachable, and efficient. It asks all the qualifying questions: "What's your budget? Are you pre-approved for a loan? What kind of home are you looking for?" These are the same questions I used to ask manually, wasting precious hours that could have been spent closing deals or strategizing for the next client.

By the time I get involved, I already know if the lead is serious and I glance at the text messages for a quick minute. I know what they're looking for, their financial situation, and whether or not they're working with another realtor. I'm not wasting time calling, texting, and emailing bad leads. I'm only engaging with people who are ready to buy or sell. I am getting serious about Buyers and Sellers using AI.

Setting It and Forgetting It
Here's where the magic happens with the old saying: **Set it and forget it!**

With my speed to lead CRM system, I'm no longer spending my days calling leads, sending emails, or trying to schedule appointments. Instead, my AI bot handles all of that. The CRM collects the information I need, books the Zoom meetings, and even sends reminders. When I walk into a meeting (or Zoom meeting), everything is ready for me—leads are pre-qualified, the client is expecting me, and I can focus on building a relationship and closing the deal.

Imagine how much time this saves. Instead of spending an entire day prospecting, and texting back and forth with 50 different people; I'm spending my time where it matters—at the closing table.

AI: The Realtor's Best Friend

Now, let's talk AI. I know the term can feel intimidating, but hear me out. AI isn't here to replace you. It's here to make your life easier. Think of it as a highly efficient assistant who never takes a day off, never gets tired, and never forgets to follow up.

Before AI, my lead generation process looked something like this: Find a potential client, spend hours trying to get them on the phone, and then more hours nurturing the relationship until they were ready to buy or sell. Now? AI does the heavy lifting for me.

I have created an AI bot that once a lead comes in, the bot introduces itself as my assistant and starts communicating with the lead in real time. Speed to Lead.

Then, it starts asking qualifying questions, and then it schedules a meeting with me and the new lead.

The first time this happened, I was ecstatic! I felt like I just unlocked a cheat code. I'm sitting here watching the texts go back and forth between the bot and the lead and I'm not doing anything! Then, it books a strategy call with the new lead and myself. During that call, we are all on the same page and soooo much time has been saved!! I know exactly what they want and we're ready to get to work more efficiently. Let's face it, most of our time is spent prospecting. This system enabled me to scale so fast that it felt like I was cheating. It still amazes me and this is just the beginning.

AI can look at market trends, analyze data, and even help with pricing strategy. It tracks local housing trends, compares them to the national market, and gives me insights on when to list a home, how to price it, and even which types of buyers are most likely to bite. This means I can offer clients more value, positioning myself as the expert who knows the market inside and out. I'm not saying to use AI to price a property but it can help give you insight to make the right strategy in very little time.

And here's the best part—while AI is handling all of this, I'm not doing anything. I can spend my time building client relationships, expanding my network, or just enjoying my day. AI isn't a gimmick—it's a game-changer. And if you're not using it, you're leaving money on the table. A lot of it. And I did this in a completely shifting market! I'm no longer the agent looking for the next deal. Now I'm the agent that everyone looks up to asking how did you do it?

Systematic Selling in Action

Let me give you a real-world example. Right now, I'm selling homes in two different states. Two. And I haven't stepped foot inside either of them. How? Technology. My buyer agents visit the houses and use Facetime/zoom to update me on-site. I'm reviewing homes with my clients remotely, pointing out cracks in ceilings or potential issues from thousands of miles away, all thanks to technology. And the best part? My clients don't care that I'm not physically there—they care that I'm efficient and getting them what they want. I have someone there so it's the best of both worlds.

By automating my lead generation, managing my communications through a CRM, and using AI to stay on top of trends and pricing, I've built a business that works without needing to be everywhere at once. I'm no longer the cog. I'm the conductor.

Why This Matters for You

Here's the thing: **You don't have to do it all.** If you're running around, trying to be everything to everyone, you're not being effective. You're just spinning your wheels. But by building a system, leveraging AI, and using technology to automate the tasks that don't require your personal touch, you free yourself up to focus on the big stuff—like closing deals and growing your business.

Selling homes systematically means you're not running on a hamster wheel. It means you're scaling your business in a way that's sustainable, profitable, and—dare I say it—enjoyable. You get your time back. You get your life back.

The real estate industry is changing fast. Those who adapt and embrace these tools will thrive. Those who don't will burn out, stuck as cogs in an outdated machine.

The Takeaway

If you want to future-proof your career, you need to stop being the cog in the system and start implementing AI tools that work for you. AI and technology are not the future—they're the present. The agents who thrive in the next decade will be the ones who master these tools now.

So, stop grinding. Build a system that works for you. Leverage AI, automate where you can, and delegate tasks that don't need your personal touch. The key is to take control of your business before it takes control of you. Honestly, this is why I'm writing this book—to show you how I reclaimed my time and made even more money in the process. Real estate can feel so overwhelming with endless tasks, but this system cuts through the noise, letting you focus on what truly matters.

CHAPTER 7:

THE NEW WAVE OF REAL ESTATE WITH AI: CRM SYSTEMS

It's a typical day, and a new lead comes in. The old way of doing things? You'd drop everything, make a phone call, send a text, or shoot over an email. You'd try to get the lead on the hook, hoping they're still interested by the time you connect with them. You might have gone back and forth a few times, chasing down information, and if you were lucky, they'd respond quickly.

But here's the reality: **The real estate game has changed.**

In today's world, everything moves faster, and realtors who aren't first to respond will lose out—plain and simple.

Whether you're managing a few leads or hundreds or even thousands, you can't afford to be the last person to follow up. This is where **AI-driven CRM systems** come into play. They're not just a luxury; they're a necessity for the modern realtor who wants to thrive.

The Role of CRM in Modern Real Estate

If you're not familiar with CRM (Customer Relationship Management) systems, let me break it down for you. Think of it as your digital assistant, your command center, and your lead tracker all in one. A good CRM system organizes your contacts, tracks every interaction, and most importantly, helps you follow up in a timely and efficient way. However, not all CRMs are created equal—when combined with AI, they become game changers.

In the past, my business ran on notebooks, spreadsheets, and a CRM that I paid a lot for. Sure, it was manageable when I was working with a handful of clients, but as my business grew, the cracks started to show. Leads slipped through the cracks, follow-ups were missed, and deals were lost simply because I couldn't keep up with the volume of work.

Fast forward to today, and all of that has changed. **The Accessible Agents CRM I created does all the heavy lifting for me and can do the same for you.** From the moment a lead comes in, it's logged into the system, and AI takes over and does all the small things that add up to hours of your day.

Speed to Lead: The Critical Factor

Let's talk about speed. There's an old saying in sales: **Speed to lead.** What this means is that the faster you contact a lead after they reach out, the higher your chances are of converting that lead into a client. Studies show that if you don't follow up with a lead within five minutes, your chances of conversion drop by 80%. Yes, **80%!** The average person won't wait around for a response—they'll move on to another faster agent.

This is where my CRM's AI comes in to play. The second a lead comes through, the CRM automatically sends a personalized message—**immediately**. We're talking within seconds. The AI takes over, introducing itself as my assistant and starting a conversation with the lead. It asks them qualifying questions like, "What neighborhood are you interested in?" or "What's your budget?"

This is not your average little bot that pops up on a website asking little questions that people get frustrated talking to. Not at all. Like I said earlier, I spent months creating this with my tech team so it would not do exactly that. This AI bot acts like my assistant and I created a professional personality for it so the leads think they are talking to my real assistant. And it is my real assistant!

It interacts with all my leads, follows up with them, and creates appointments for me.

By the time I step into the conversation, the lead is pre-qualified, and I already know whether or not they're serious. That's the magic of **AI-driven CRM**—it automates the front-end work, freeing up my time to focus on building relationships and closing deals.

A CRM System that Works for You

So, how does the Accessible Agents CRM really work? It's more than just a fancy tool—it's an automated system designed to handle the heavy lifting so you can focus on closing deals. Here's how I've set mine up to run like a well-oiled machine:

1. **Lead Enters the System**: The moment someone reaches out through my website, social media, or any real estate advertisement, that lead is automatically entered into my CRM. No manual input is required. This is where automation kicks in. Whether it's a random inquiry or someone seriously interested, the system captures their details and immediately adds them to my database. From there, the real magic begins.

2. **Immediate Response**: The moment the lead hits the system, an AI-driven response is sent out

on my behalf. And no–it doesn't sound robotic. I spent months with my team fine-tuning this bot to sound personable and engaging. It's like having a digital assistant that knows how to ask the right questions without feeling impersonal. Questions like, "What kind of property are you looking for?" and "Are you pre-approved for a home loan?" get the lead engaged with the system instantly, giving me crucial information right off the bat without me having to spend my time pre-qualifying the leads over and over again

3. **Qualifying the Lead**: Based on the answers they provide, the CRM then starts categorizing the leads. If they're serious buyers—let's say they're pre-approved and actively searching for homes—they're automatically bumped up the priority list. If they're just browsing or aren't ready to buy yet, the system nurtures them by keeping in touch, sending them useful information, and gently guiding them along until they're ready to take the next step. This way, no lead falls through the cracks.

4. **Booking a Meeting**: Once the lead reaches a point where they're ready to get serious, the CRM takes the next step and automatically schedules a meeting. This could be a Zoom meeting to view

properties virtually, a face to face meeting, or a phone call. Either way, the system has already done the legwork in getting me face-to-face (or screen-to-screen) with the client. It's seamless, saving me time and ensuring the client feels taken care of.

5. **Follow-Up and Reminders**: One of the best parts of having a robust CRM is that it never forgets. Throughout the process, it sends out automatic follow-up messages to keep the lead engaged. From reminders about upcoming meetings to personalized check-ins, the system handles it all. I never have to worry about forgetting to check in or if someone slipped off my radar—the CRM keeps everything organized and running smoothly.

AI and the Personal Touch

Here's where some realtors start to worry: "Won't my clients know it's a bot? Won't they feel like they're dealing with a machine instead of a human?" Not if you do it right—and not with the system my team and I created, which helped me become the number one agent in Texas at my brokerage. The key is striking the perfect balance between automation and maintaining that personal, human touch. When done properly, AI can enhance your client interactions without ever making them feel impersonal.

The key to using AI in your CRM is to give it a **personality**. When I first set up my CRM, I spent time crafting the messages so they didn't feel robotic. I wanted my AI assistant to sound like a real person—polite, professional, and helpful. The result? Clients don't feel like they're talking to a machine; they feel like they're getting great service from my team. I've had clients compliment "Erica," my AI assistant, on how responsive and friendly she is. Little do they know, Erica is a bot.

If you still think this is strange, I have also set up a feature where I can watch, in real-time, the texts going back and forth between my bot and the lead. It's amazing! I might be cooking and then my phone starts texting back and forth with a client. I will watch it sometimes and make sure it's doing a good job. Then, after a while of going back and forth with the lead, my meeting is booked and I have a full schedule of meetings.

Scaling Your Business with AI

One of the biggest advantages of using an AI-driven CRM system is **scalability**. When I was managing everything manually, there was a limit to how many clients I could handle. I was constantly juggling my time between following up with leads, showing homes, and managing all of the everyday nuances of owning your own business like paperwork, tech, CE courses, etc.

But now? **I can scale without adding more hours to my day.**

With my CRM handling lead generation, follow-ups, and scheduling, I can manage ten times the number of clients I used to. It allows me to grow my business without sacrificing quality or burning out. I'm able to focus on what matters—closing deals and providing top-notch service—while the system takes care of the rest. It always puts a big smile on my face when I'm in a meeting with a client and I see my phone is having a conversation with a new client without me. What an amazing feeling!

The Benefits of Automation

Automation is more than just a time-saver, it's a game-changer. By integrating it into your CRM system, you're not only streamlining your processes, but you're also improving the overall experience for your clients. Let's break down how:

1. **Never Miss a Lead**: No more leads slipping through the cracks because you failed to follow up. One of the most valuable aspects of automation is lead tracking. With a CRM, every interaction with a potential client is automatically recorded, ensuring that no lead falls through the cracks. Whether it's a follow-up email or a nudge to remind them of an upcoming meeting, the

system ensures that every lead is engaged until you either close the deal or explicitly say no. This eliminates the human error that comes with manually tracking leads, preventing that dreaded realization that you overlooked a promising lead

2. **Stay Organized**: Every contact, every conversation, every task—it's all logged in the CRM. You never have to worry about losing a sticky note or forgetting who said what.

3. **Improve Client Relationships**: People want to feel like they're getting your personal attention, even when they know you're busy. With an AI-driven CRM, that becomes a reality. The system sends out timely follow-ups, reminders, and check-ins on your behalf, making it seem like you're always tailoring things according to your client's needs. Your clients will feel valued and appreciated, and you'll maintain strong relationships without the manual effort. And let's be honest—consistent, meaningful contact is the key to securing lifelong clients and repeat business.

4. **Close Deals Faster**: one of the biggest advantages of automation is that it speeds up the sales cycle. Instead of wasting time manually qualifying leads or scheduling meetings, the

system takes care of the heavy lifting. By the time you step in, the lead has been qualified, their preferences noted, and a meeting scheduled—all without you having to manually handle any of it. This leaves you with more time to focus on what you do best: closing the deal.

5. **Optimize Your Time**: Let's face it—most of us didn't get into real estate to manage spreadsheets and send follow-up emails all day. Automation frees you from the mundane, administrative tasks that can easily be handled by AI. With those routine tasks off your plate, you can focus on what moves the needle: building relationships, strategizing for growth, and negotiating deals. Essentially, automation allows you to scale your business without losing the personal touch that makes you successful.

AI in Real Estate: The Future is Now

The real estate industry is changing, and AI is leading the way. Realtors who embrace this technology now will be the ones thriving in the future. If you're still doing everything manually, you're going to fall behind.

AI-driven CRM systems allow you to provide better service, stay on top of leads, and scale your business without burning out. You'll never miss a follow-up, never forget a lead, and never feel overwhelmed by the volume of work again.

AI won't replace you—it will enhance you. It's a tool that allows you to focus on what really matters: building relationships, closing deals, and growing your business. And isn't that what we all want?

And not only is it a great tool for your CRM but it also enhances your day-to-day work! As I was saying earlier in the book, it can do a lot of other things for you too in order to free up even more time. These items are also being integrated into my CRM.

The Takeaway

In today's fast-paced world, **speed to lead** is critical. If you're not using a CRM system that integrates AI, you're missing out on one of the most powerful tools available to modern realtors. With AI handling the repetitive tasks, you can focus on providing personalized service and scaling your business. That's why I created Accessible Agents!

Automation isn't just the future—it's the present. If you want to thrive in the new wave of real estate, it's time to embrace AI and let it work for you. After all, isn't it time you stopped working harder and started working smarter?

CHAPTER 8:

COMPREHENSIVE SUMMARY AND INSIGHTS

As we close this journey, it's crucial to bring together the lessons from previous chapters and explore how a comprehensive understanding can truly future-proof your real estate career. Success in real estate requires more than just the basics; it demands a thorough grasp of market dynamics, customer behavior and industry shifts. In this chapter, we'll tie these concepts together and dive into trade secrets that can offer you a competitive edge.

Engaging with Customers and Markets

To truly thrive in real estate, you need to go beyond simply understanding your clients—you must also stay connected to the ever evolving market. Success comes from mastering both sides: knowing exactly what your clients need and being prepared to pivot when the market shifts. This involves not just reacting to changes but anticipating them by analyzing trends, studying economic indicators, and keeping a close eye on the factors that drive supply and demand. Staying informed is what keeps you competitive, adaptable, and always ahead of the curve. This right here is one way of how being a good Realtor compares to being a not so good Realtor.

Understanding Customer Needs:
By keeping the client at the center of your strategy, you'll build loyalty and long-term relationships. Engaged customers are more likely to refer others and return when they're ready to buy or sell again.

Adapting to Market Shifts:
As discussed earlier, the market can shift like a weather vane in a hurricane. By staying informed and agile, you can anticipate changes and adjust your strategies to remain relevant and effective. This includes bringing AI into your business and other items that you may not know how to implement but need to stay ahead of the curve.

A Realtor's Trade Secret: Leveraging the Bell Curve and 80/20 Rule

One trade secret that has proven effective across industries is applying the bell curve and the 80/20 rule (or Pareto Principle). In real estate, this means focusing on the 20% of activities that will yield 80% of the results. For example, a small portion of your client base—typically repeat clients and referrals—often generates the largest net income. By identifying and nurturing these key relationships, you can maximize your efforts and focus on what truly drives success.

The bell curve, which shows a distribution of results, is also essential. At one end, you have the top-performing agents, and at the other, those struggling. By studying the traits and strategies of top performers, you can replicate their success. In your business, identify where your activities fall on this curve and work to shift more towards the high-performance end.

Recognizing Early Warning Signals in Market Dynamics

Understanding how various industries interact can provide early warning signals when change is on the horizon. Economic shifts often ripple through sectors in a recognizable pattern, allowing you to anticipate upcoming challenges or opportunities. When you notice a slump or economic challenge in one industry, you can mentally calculate the probable impact on other industries. These sectors don't just interact—they generally follow a consistent sequence:

Industrial → Oil and Gas → Utility → Manufacturing → Food and Beverage → Construction → Wholesale → Retail → Consumer Products.

For instance, if a downturn begins in the oil and gas sector, it will likely impact utilities next, followed by manufacturing, and so forth. Recognizing this sequence allows you to prepare and strategize before the effects reach your area of focus. Similarly, when new technology emerges, its initial impact is often seen in consumer products, and the influence moves backward through the sequence. By tracking these shifts, you can position yourself to adapt in advance.

The Evolution of Technology, Seasonality, and Workloads

Real estate is not static. As technology evolves, so do customer expectations and the seasonality of demand:

Technology Evolution: AI, CRM systems, and data analytics are transforming how realtors engage with clients and close deals. Those who embrace these tools will find it easier to stay ahead of the competition. This is exactly why I created my proven CRM with AI technology called

Accessible Agents which has generated millions in sales and helped me become the number one agent in Texas.

Seasonality of Demand: Different seasons bring varying demand levels. By understanding these cycles, you can prepare your marketing and outreach strategies accordingly, maximizing high-demand periods and staying productive during slower months.

Company Workloads: Just as with seasonality, internal workloads can fluctuate. Managing your time and resources effectively ensures that your team remains efficient without burnout.

Tying Concepts Together

Understanding these elements in isolation is helpful, but the real power comes when you see how they interact. Market dynamics, for instance, follow the same principles as those seen in other industries. If you were to place different industries on the same line of market dynamics, you would likely observe similar patterns in supply and demand changes. Consider the real estate industry alongside tech: both are influenced by seasonality, both can benefit from the 80/20 rule, and both have top performers who set the standard for others.

Example: Supply Chain Adaptation

Imagine a supply chain that adapts to changes in technology. As advancements are made, supply increases, and costs decrease. In real estate, we can see similar trends. When market conditions are favorable, such as low interest rates, the supply of homes might increase as more people look to sell or buy. By understanding these shifts, you can better predict market trends and adjust your strategies to be in the right place at the right time.

The Future-Proof Realtor

To be truly future-proof, you must continually adapt and apply these concepts. By staying engaged with clients, leveraging technology, and understanding the deeper patterns that drive success, you can thrive even when market dynamics shift. Analyzing these trends and recognizing the sequential impacts can offer you an anticipatory edge, enabling you to navigate upcoming challenges with foresight and flexibility. By integrating these lessons, you not only prepare yourself for today's challenges but also position yourself as a resilient, forward-thinking professional ready for whatever the future holds.

CHAPTER 9:

JOIN THE TEAM: WHY BEING PART OF THE RIGHT AGENCY MAKES ALL THE DIFFERENCE

Real estate can be a tough, isolating career. You're an independent contractor, often fending for yourself in an industry where the competition is fierce, and the training is minimal. Most brokerages hand you a contract, say "Best Of Luck" and send you on your way. But here's the problem with that: **If you're constantly going it alone, you'll never grow.**

That's the key difference between being part of a **team** that supports your growth and being just another cog in the machine. When you're part of a forward-thinking agency that wants you to thrive, the game changes. And that's exactly what we offer. This isn't your run-of-the-mill brokerage or team, where the focus is solely on churning out sales—this is about building something bigger and better, together. Of course, sales is a major part of it and we offer some of the best coaching. We also talk about your goals and how you can hit the financial number you are reaching for.

The Difference Between Us and Them

Let's break it down. Most traditional brokerages are about one thing: **sales, sales, sales.** They're focused on teaching you how to read contracts, host open houses, and close deals. That's all well and good, but here's the truth: **They're not invested in you in the slightest.** They want you to sell homes, meet quotas, and move on to the next deal. You're hustling day in and day out, but no matter how hard you grind, it feels like you're always stuck in the same spot.

It's frustrating, right? You're pouring time and energy into deals that keep you busy but never truly free. It's like you're always chasing, but never catching up. Sure, you can close deals, and get a commission but where's the growth? Where's the path to something bigger? They're not focused on helping you build a lasting business, just squeezing one more sale out of you until you're done.

At our agency, we take a different approach. We don't want you to just sell homes—we want to help you **build a thriving business** that's scalable and sustainable. Of course, if you want to sell property and not build a big business, this team is still for you because you'll have more time on your hands and more money to prove it. We've got the tools, systems, and real mentorship to help you build something sustainable. No more spinning your wheels. We give you the structure and support to grow without burning out. Imagine having your own AI assistant booking calls for you and your closing agreements with motivated sellers!

And this is exactly why I wrote this book and created the team I have created! I spun my wheels and kept looking for the next deal but what was I building? What was my goal? What was my big why? And who was going to help me get there? Honestly? No one was helping me get there. They just wanted me to get another sale. And I wanted another sale. And another and another but I also wanted to figure out a smoother process to get that next sale. And I figured it out! And when I did, it was a game changer.

I've worked at other brokerages that promised the world, but once I signed up, I was left in the dark, constantly asking things like "When is the meeting? Where? Oh, I thought we were talking about X and not Y." It was chaotic and lacked structure. I built this because I wanted to offer what I never received—a streamlined process, real support, hands-on coaching, and state of the art technology. I've spent thousands each month learning and understanding the game. Now it's time for me to pass my knowledge on as a number one agent in one of the biggest states at one of the biggest brokerages. I still can't believe I became the number one agent in Texas. All thanks to my previous knowledge of real estate and creating the right tools with the newest technology available.

This team that I helped build not only focuses on creating what you want to create but also coaches you on how to close those difficult transactions and helps you learn the true insides and outs of the real estate industry. Real estate is not simply about opening doors and writing a contract. Anyone can do that and that's why a lot of people get their license. They see the TV shows, they think it's easy, and they see that it's not too difficult to study and get the license. They get the license and are thrown to the wolves wondering, "what the heck is this industry? This is NOTHING like it is on TV." That's right! It is nothing like on TV. It's tough to even make one sale. I get it. I remember my first sale and I'm sure you do too.

There is so much red tape in real estate that deals fall apart. I like to think of myself as one of the best people to keep deals together. There are so many stories I can tell of a transaction I was involved in where the Buyer or Seller simply wanted to get out. But if you know what types of questions to ask and how to navigate real estate, I promise you that you can most likely keep that transaction together and not spin your wheels trying to find another house for your buyer or another buyer for your seller. My coaching talks about all of this and helps you learn the real tools inside the industry. This type of coaching mixed with the AI tools I've created in my Speed to Lead AI system, it's game over. You'll have everything you need at your fingertips to succeed.

THE "GOOD DIRT" CONCEPT: IT'S ALL ABOUT GROWTH

You've probably heard the saying, "The grass is greener where you water it." But what's equally important is the **dirt**—the foundation you plant yourself in. If you're working in bad soil, no amount of water is going to help you grow. That's where most brokerages fall short— they're not giving you the environment to truly thrive.

At our agency, we've created what I like to call "good dirt." It's a foundation that's built on **support, mentorship, and cutting-edge tools and technology**. You're not just handed a stack of papers and told to figure it out. You're given access to a network of experienced agents, continuous training, and the most advanced technology in the world. All from myself and other top Realtors in the country! This is where real growth happens.

The Tools That Set Us Apart

One of the biggest differences between us and other brokerages is the **technology** we provide. Most agencies give you a basic website and maybe a CRM, but they don't show you how to use it effectively. They certainly don't teach you how to leverage AI or automated systems to grow your business.

Here's what we offer:

1. **AI-Driven Accessible Agents CRM System**: As we talked about in the last chapter, our CRM isn't just a tool for storing contacts. It's an intelligent system that helps you gain new leads, track leads, automate follow-ups, and close deals faster than I can say SOLD. It is one of the key tools that helped me get to where I am today.. With this, you're not spending your time managing data—you're letting the system work for you and spending your time where it matters, closing the deals.

2. **Trackable Emails:** Imagine sending an email and wondering—did the client even open it? What if you missed an opportunity because they clicked, but you didn't follow up? That could cost you a deal. But with our system, you'll know exactly when they engage. If they click the link, it

triggers a follow-up sequence instantly. And the best part? It's all in one CRM. No more juggling 5-10 platforms, losing time and potentially losing clients. You stay ahead, and your business runs like clockwork.

3. **Your Dedicated Phone Number:** The AI system uses a completely different phone number that is associated only with you. And you can track everything from it. Texts, phone calls, notes made, whatever you want or don't want. Our custom-built CRM has been a game-changer for our success, and we're ready to pass it on to you.

4. **Proven Systems for Consistent Lead Flow**: Unlike many brokerages that expect you to figure out lead generation on your own, we provide you with proven systems for generating leads. Whether it's through digital marketing, social media, or AI-driven ads, we give you the tools and training to ensure you always have a full pipeline of potential clients. Want to learn how I used this CRM to take me to the number one agent in Texas? I provide the coaching. Want to learn how to utilize YouTube and generate free inbound leads? We got you covered with the best YouTube Realtors out there. Want to know how to integrate more AI into your business? We not

only teach it, we implement it and show you how to use it! I have tried to make this as easy and effortless as possible because I understand how difficult it can be.

5. **Effortlessly Automated Marketing Tools**: Say goodbye to micromanaging every detail of your marketing campaigns. Our automated tools streamline the entire process—creating, managing, and tracking campaigns seamlessly across multiple platforms. That means your message is always hitting the right audience at the right time without the hassle. You simply talk to the leads that are pre-qualified with our AI driven Speed to Lead Software and then with our coaching, we will teach you how to close the deal and manage the transaction.

6. **Cloud-Based Support, Anytime, Anywhere**: With our cloud-based brokerage, you won't be left in the dust. Need help? Your team of brokers, trainers, and mentors are just a click away. Do you have a contract question? Head into the virtual office and get a full walk-through in minutes. No more chasing down your principal broker—support is now fast, reliable, and always within reach. So you're never riding solo on this journey, partner.

The Power of Community

Let's be honest: real estate can be a lonely road. You're out there hustling, building your reputation, and securing deals—all on your own. But that changes when you're part of the right team. You're not just another agent in a sea of agents—you're part of a supportive network invested in your success. At Accessible Agents and Rowdy Realtor Nation, the community isn't just a buzzword, it's the backbone of everything we do.

We foster a collaborative culture, where agents support each other's growth. We exchange insights, strategies, and tips to strengthen our businesses together. Here, competition isn't the focus—when one of us grows, we all grow.

Real Training, Real Mentorship

Here's where we set ourselves apart: We don't just hand you tools and leave you to figure it out. A lot of brokerages will toss you a CRM and some materials, say "good luck," and call it a day. But not here. We go further because we care about your success. We provide **real** training and coaching from agents who've walked in your shoes and know what it takes to succeed.

From hands-on workshops to one-on-one coaching, we guide you step by step, ensuring you don't just have the tools, but that you know how to use them to grow your business. Whether you're fresh to the industry or a seasoned pro, there's always room to improve, and we're here to support your growth at every turn.

Building a Lasting Business, Not Just a Job

Here's the real game-changer: we're not just teaching you to sell homes—we're helping you build a business that works for you, even when you're not working. Most brokerages push for one deal after another, but we're here to set you up for lasting success.

With us, you'll create systems that scale effortlessly, automate routine tasks, and lay a rock-solid foundation for future income. Imagine a business that grows itself, freeing you to focus on bigger dreams and things that truly matter to you. Whether it's spending more time with your family or building a lasting legacy. Something you can look back on with pride, knowing you've built something that stands the test of time. I am also a Certified Real Estate Negotiator and will help you negotiate the best deals so you become a hero for your clients!

The Incentives You Can't Get Anywhere Else

What truly sets us apart is our incentive structure. While most brokerages only offer commissions, we go further—we help you build long-term wealth for your family and for your retirement. Like I said earlier, if I had joined this team at the beginning, I would be better off now. Why?

At our agency, you're not just earning commissions—you're building long-term wealth. By simply doing what you do best, selling homes, you can earn stock in the company. These stock incentives function like a built-in retirement plan, allowing your hard work today to keep paying dividends in the future. It's better than just making immediate income, you get to build a stable and secure stream of income for years to follow. Every transaction contributes to your future, giving you a tangible stake in the company's growth while ensuring your efforts continue to pay off even after the sale is closed.

But that's just the beginning. You also have the opportunity to mentor and attract new agents, creating more income as they build their own businesses. This is not about working harder, it's about working smarter, building multiple streams of income, and securing your financial future. With us, you're building wealth that lasts.

On top of that, you also have the capability to earn your commission split/cap rate back! And this is one big reason why I said I would be better off because if I had simply joined and not done anything different, I would have received my cap rate back almost every year and had that back in my pocket or even better, into rewarding stocks.

We also offer commercial real estate opportunities so the options are endless as to what type of real estate you want to sell. I once came across a client that had a commercial building while I was at another brokerage and my brokerage would not help me. Furthermore, the brokerage said I had to give that transaction to their commercial department because I was only a residential Realtor and could not handle commercial. What? But I have a real estate license. Not a "Residential" Real Estate license. I can sell whatever real estate I want. Yes, and here there are no boundaries.

I have sold everything from large commercial buildings, to luxury penthouses, luxury homes, to helping investors build their portfolios, first time home buyers, manufactured homes, even raw land. You name it, I've sold it in real estate. And this is the type of coaching I bring to you. With my expertise in all of these fields, I will help you succeed because that is my passion and I feel that I owe it to the real estate industry to help lead and create the Future Proof Realtors.

Why Join Us?

Why make the leap? Why leave your current brokerage or team to come here, or invest in our system? The truth is, you're probably feeling stuck. Maybe you're working harder than ever but barely seeing growth. Maybe your current brokerage promises support but leaves you to figure everything out on your own. Maybe you feel like you're paying too much into their system and not getting enough in return. You're tired of the grind—of constantly chasing the next deal, unsure if you'll ever truly build something that lasts.

Here's the reality: most agents plateau because they're missing one thing—**real support**. You need more than just a place to hang your license. You need systems that work, mentorship that's real, and a community that's dedicated to your success. It's frustrating to watch others thrive while you're spinning your wheels, knowing you're capable of so much more.

That's where we come in. When you join us, you're not just getting another job—you're stepping into an ecosystem designed for **your growth and success**. We provide the tools, the training, and the community to help you break free from that cycle and start building a business that can scale. And here's the best part: we'll give you our proven system free when you become part of our team, ensuring you're not just selling homes—you're building wealth, creating freedom, and operate the business you've always wanted. And most importantly, you're positioning yourself to build a business that can weather any market, thrive in any economy, and continue growing year after year.

You've worked hard, but now it's time to work smart—on your terms, with the right support behind you. Ready to level up? We're here to make it happen.

The Takeaway

The difference between a mediocre real estate career and a thriving business boils down to one key factor: **The team you're part of and what they offer.** At our agency, we don't just teach you how to sell homes—we teach you how to sell homes efficiently while utilizing the latest technology to build a business that lasts. And this is all built by seasoned agents who have seen a lot out in the field. Not from people who just know a little about tech. Or have sold a few houses. Oh no, we've got real estate covered—we know all the ins and outs and exactly what's happening in the industry from all our sources. We give you the tools, the training, and the support you need to thrive in today's market and tomorrow's.

If you're done being just another agent, and you're ready to step into real growth, it's time to join a community that's invested in your success. Let's build something incredible together. Let us help you escape the race of having to chase deals 24/7 and future-proof your real estate career.

Become a part of Accessible Agents and the Rowdy Realtor Nation today and watch your business thrive by learning from some of the best, and getting the most technologically advanced AI real estate CRM system out there!

Check us out at AccessibleAgents.com if you're ready to skyrocket your real estate career.

Martin Tijmes.

www.ingramcontent.com/pod-product-compliance
Lightning Source LLC
Chambersburg PA
CBHW071055240526
45469CB00006BD/2313